THORNS
AND
ROSES

The stories of our lives

THORNS
AND
ROSES

The stories of our lives

UJU ORAMAH
Cover and sketches by Chike Oramah
Edited by Lucy Azubuike

DivineChild Publishers
Nashville, Tennessee

DEDICATION

To my mom, the Late Mrs. Elizabeth Azubuike Odimegwu— a woman who sacrificed her dreams in order to let her children have theirs.

TABLE OF CONTENT

TABLE OF CONTENT

AUTHOR'S NOTE

Some thoughts are conceived, but never get to form fully.
Many are forgotten as soon as they begin to develop.
Others, though born, never see the daylight. Many thoughts
delivered years ago, still live and breathe.

These words that flow on each page of this book are the
collection of my thoughts about change, life, nature, and
aging. These words have flown through me through time.

There is a child in every one of us that needs attention. That
child cries for affection and reaches out for recognition. That
child needs to be hugged, kissed, and loved. When this baby
in us is satisfied, we are saved from depression! It is crucial
to pay attention to this child in all of us who helps us to age
gracefully and be in tune with ourselves, others, and nature.

Nature offers limitless treasures: ocean, wind, rain, hills,
valleys, trees, etc.

Once we allow the child in us to explore and appreciate
nature, we are bound to enjoy immeasurable feelings of bliss.

Uju Oramah
Nashville, Tennessee
2017

THORNS AND ROSES

Co-exist
One doesn't exist without the other
So are struggles and victories, pains and joys, life and death
You can't have it any other way
Thus
You can't experience deep joy without struggle
You can't have life without death
By being alive, you have accepted to die
To die means that you lived
You can't separate death from life
Neither can you separate life from death
We make both count by the way we live, and by the way we die

ACKNOWLEDGMENTS

I thank God Almighty for his providence and wisdom that make this book a reality.

My sincere appreciations go to all the people that assisted me in the making of this book. My special thanks go to Tina Rogers, Isidore Nkwocha, Liz Dudas, Udo Obodo, Candace Thomas, and Mrs. Lewis. To many others whose names are not listed here. I say thank you

Above all, I want to thank Lucy Azubuike and my hubby, Chike Oramah, for their immense support

PREFACE

Everything changes.
With change, nothing is guaranteed and nothing is like it seems.
It is said that "the only constant thing is change."
Hence, how do humans face these transition challenges from birth to death?
These poems are snapshots of my personal journey as I seek to understand our world, human nature, and these changes.

WONDERLAND

On a hill, dense in scented flowers
Adorable and uncommon
Its perfume teases
I stood, grinning cheek to cheek
Fully tantalized
Consuming every moment
No worries, no fears
Calm breeze kissing the flowers
And, kissing me
Looking up at the sky
Suddenly- so blue, so enchanting
Spreading my hands
Whirling and twirling, round and round
It is magic
It intoxicates
It's reality, I embrace

LIFE IS BEAUTIFUL

It's wonderful to be alive
Taking in and releasing air— priceless
Watching the sunset— a privilege
Meeting the dawn — a treat
Watching the birds fly and sing— a thrill
Pit-a-pat, my heart beats
Like keynotes, everything falls into rhythm
Mother cuddles her crying baby
While the gentle breeze caresses the child with her mother's
long hair
With gaiety, men walk by with their women
Children build castles in the red sand
Unconsciously, I conjure up my childhood
Nostalgic feelings envelop me
On a brick fence, an Agama lizard stiffly protects its territory
Cars of different shapes and makes hustle by
Suddenly my body is wet; it is raining
No one seems to mind
Women, though, plug banana leaves to shade their hair
Now, it is evening; food time
Cauldron boiling to the brim
Burning firewood emits exotic fragrances
Deliciously coating the air
Air filled with merriments
People hugging and kissing
Discussing, chanting
I see my life running
I see lives running with mine
I've seen my different looks, and the world's
The changes are several and continuous
Life is beautiful; it's worth living
Simply look around; nothing shortchanges it
At sunset, my hands are weak

Suddenly like a vegetable, I drift toward sleep
Unwillingly, I close my eyes
I wait for the new dawn
Soon, it will be here
The rhythm of life ceaselessly plays anew
Life indeed is beautiful!

THE STARS

I look at the sky
Sparkling lights glow down on me
My eyes roam the sky
Counting its numerous stars
One to thousands
I gradually feel the nudging pain
On my burdened neck
I look down after counting the thousands of stars
To see myself so far from home
I turn and run
Still in the euphoria of the celestial body
Abundantly scattered above
I wonder how much these stars would cost if the human could possess them?

ANONYMOUS GIRL

She is seventeen, with dove-like appearance
But she is a cat and walks like one, too
She misses nothing
Hair is kept short, with face and legs to die for
She whispers like a breeze to unusual company
But is a parrot; she misses nothing
Timid, but lovely; an angel, strangers conclude
How wrong! How naive! I laugh, in silence
They are deceived; she misses nothing
All events stick to her like glue
She re-echoes them to those you least expect
You might wonder who she is
I which I could tell you
For she's Anonymous

CHIDIMMA

Oh, baby, delicate but active
Lay quietly sound asleep
Oblivious of your surroundings
Ever smiling face
Smiling at the world, even while asleep
Now I stand, watching you sleep, I itch to cuddle you
No
I must let you be
My willing hand and heart
Ache to rock you a while
Oh! no!
I must let you be
Sleep on, sweet baby, for your tomorrow will be bright
I know this sleep will give you strength to conquer all that
Crosses your way
Sleep on, sweet baby
For tomorrow, you and I will play to our heart's content

A MEDIUM

Living— a thing to be proud of
Death— a thing to dread
Human think before you judge
Living— a complex thing to handle
Death— a complex thing that defeats
Human think before you choose
Living—limited
Death—unlimited
Human a medium for their operation
Human, do you have a choice?

A SNAKE IT SHOULD BE

Early morning as I sleep
Gentle push, I feel on my body
My eyes open
I behold my friend shaking in fear
What's the matter?
Her hand points to the window
Jumping from my bed, I run for the door
She follows
Out we go shouting for help
Snake! Snake! We exclaim
"It's a cobra!" a neighbor shouts
Our hostel, now, in a state of chaos
Neighbors running helter-skelter
Armed with sticks and rods
Bravely they make for the window
Determined, they open the window
Mysteriously, nothing is found
Where has it gone? We stand in horror
What to make of it? No one can answer
It reappears!
The bravest stabs it with a stick
She caught the snake! Everyone breathed a sigh of relief
But suddenly
Laughter filled the air
Why the laughter, you might wonder?
The snake
The horrible cobra
Is just a neglected cobweb!

AGING

I wonder how kindly aging will treat me
My eyes, can you see me to my end?
The scent of roses, will you still cause me to smile and to
Dance?
My limbs, can I walk and wave with you?
How roughly will the wrinkles adorn me?
The future generation's ideas—will I flow with them?
My cherished dreams, will you be realized?
These thoughts haunt my mind
All I priced so high
What will become of them when my senses fail?

TOMORROW EVER COMES

Today was tomorrow of yesterday
A day after tomorrow, the day before yesterday
Plans were made.
Today is here, making mockery of all plans made yesterday
Yet one continues to make plans, hoping for tomorrow to
Come
"If tomorrow comes, if it could just come fast!"
But when today came, it was found that tomorrow never
Comes
Does tomorrow ever come?

OH! HUMAN!

You suddenly exist
Knowing not from where you appeared, nor to where you would
Disappear
Having just what you hear and see as guide
You grab all you can and fight for some more
You lord in the ocean you know not. With belief, you are in
Control
When life's waves come calling
You are ruffled and tossed up and down
You fly like a dry leaf in the wind
When life waves give you a break
You dust yourself up and continue to grab and acquire
Pretending once again that you are in control

HOW MANY MILES?

How many miles can I walk before my end?
An unending journey that takes me to my end
I wake up and I walk on
Life is said to be a journey
And I'll walk to my end

DREAM

Dream, you have occupied our days!
Young and old continue to trust you
You act as hope for all
We stick to you
Rather than live
Like a baby, you are conceived
Your birth is stopped most times
By a hand of fate
Longer than ours
It either aborts you
Or you become stillborn
But we continue to await

DAYS OF YESTERYEARS

In meditation
I conjured up the days gone by
Oh, my childhood—the innocent days
The yesteryears
How I long for you
The time when nothing mattered!
The world was there for me
Like a planted seed
I've grown
Matured
Tiptoeing towards my grave
Oh, my yesteryears!
Though you've gone
I know you existed
And still, exist —within me

POWER TILL DEATH DO US PART

Sounds of victory vibrates all around
'We've won', we're independent'
Echoes and re-echoes
Like a dream, mother African children get freed
The whites have been booted out
But then
African tyrants usher in
The scene as in the book, "Animal Farm,"
metamorphosed into mourning
Scepter reeks of corruption
Mismanagement, betrayal, fraud …
Coups like pendulum swing
Ornamented with empty promises
Democracy becomes 'demo-crazy'
Charles Taylor, Idi Amin, Sani Abacha…
Vultures, in unison, beat the drum of 'demo-crazy'
Power intoxicates!
Power, till death do us part!

CHEER UP

You are gloomy and forlorn
You are a shadow of your yesterday
But yesterday you were all smiles and charming
What tragedy transformed you
Cheer up! This too shall pass

DIAMOND BELT

What a beautiful woman
With diamond belt around her waist
Yet, a thin rag wraps her and her baby
Her quivering hand holds her plate
Outstretched for alms
Teardrops fall unguided, down her beautiful face
Her skeletal baby strapped loosely at her back
He Wails
His fingers are his feeding bottle
For mama's breast is out of milk
His sisters lay still, old enough to see mama's pain
They die slowly at her feet
Cold shivers run down my spine
What spell traps this woman?
What spell banished her to perpetual slavery?
Within her extreme poverty
Lies unexploited, infinite wealth
The envy of all whom she asks for help

THE ROADSIDE TENT

A man
Walks up and down
Sells oranges
No education
No hope of being educated
Having only his native tongue
His only means of communication
He walks quite a distance to make a sale
Around the town, he merrily goes
Looking for a chance to make a sale
All over the town, he anxiously goes
Looking for a break-through
His feet protected by tattered slippers
His legs coated with dust
The only stockings he ever wore
Each day, the cycle is repeated
Days and years come and go
Tired now, from stress and age
Helpless to help himself
No help anywhere in sight
He makes a tent by the road
One night he sleeps and never wakes
The roadside tent, his final resting place

BLEEDING HEART

The heart yearns, like a deer for running water
Engraved with deep scars that drip fresh blood
Silently; no eyes notice the wound that breathes
And lashes the bearer, forcing tears to flow unguided
The heart longs to live
Thirsts to be alive
Hopes for a cure

TSUNAMI

I see the years gone by like lost waves
I hear my laughter echoing in my past
The best moments and times
When life smiled lovingly at me
Now, I feel my tears running freely for the beclouded days
Of unending mourning and wailing
Without succor, without hope
Now, I live my life between laughter and sorrow
My eyes open to an unending fact of life
Laughter and tears are still in the future
These realities hit me ceaselessly
I welcome the laughter that is to be mine
Yet am dead with fear of sorrows of the future
I wish them away, but wishes are not horses
Look at Tsunami Asia
No one saw it coming
Sweet-water rains freely down my face
I see the future from the present
Pregnant with mysteries and puzzles
That will, on one hand, pamper us
And on another, beat and leave us wailing
I look behind me, unconsciously shielding my eyes
From the miseries and inexplicable pain
That has mercilessly beaten Southeast Asia
Taking in its wake, her voice and sweat
In its fury, her most cherished possessions
Her flesh and blood

RUTHLESS

Our world is veiled in secrecy
The answers to questions incomplete
Creating a house, instead of a home
A suffocating cage instead of a free ground
A stage for oppressors in place of liberators
The ruthless wins over and over
A hammer exerts at will for power brokers
Toothless dog, re-echoes songs of wolves
Empty promises
Generations are stripped
Left for death
Rags become their royal robes
Leftovers; their food
Justice, where is your sword?
Life, a misery for the downtrodden
Life, a terror for the voiceless

AGONY

Living, breathing, but caged
Hoping, waiting, but nothing
Bored, all tears- an excruciating misery

HE IS A MAN

I notice his movement
Am I in a trance?
I wipe off my facial sweat
He looks like an offshoot of expired youth
He is like a bone, bagged in a layer of skin
Goosebumps cover my body
I step backward, nearly wetting my pants in panic
I open my mouth; no word came
The bone, at a snail's pace, moves toward me
Two nuts in place of eyeballs stare at me
Flies chorus after him
Fruitlessly, his hands could not scare them away
I stand hypnotized, blank
No reasonable thought came
"A ghost?" my mind whispers
Rooted to the spot, I remain
Each of his steps is tortured
Suddenly, he stops
Painfully he sits down and looks at me
He opens his mouth; no word formed
Tears run down his battered face
Loosened from my stupor, I reach out to him
He slumps forward into my arms
I hold him close
He smiles and sleeps a nd never wakes

YESTERDAY AND YEARS

I see you crying
Letting out the pent-up pain
Your tears clear the bile that abides in you for ages
You are crying not just for today's event
But for what yesterday has taken away forever
You are still crying
Emptying from your life
The pillars of pain
Erected and watered by time
You are fading fast right before my eyes
Now you have aged
By wounds of yesteryears

SPOT THE DIFFERENCE

What's the difference between human and beast?
A beast kills because it's hungry
Human kills to show power
Beast does not waste food
Human is proud to waste
Beast eats to satisfaction and leaves for others
Human feasts and squanders amongst poverty
Beast is its kind's keeper
Human is his kind's killer
Beast is said to be wild
Beast and human, who is wild?
Beast and human, who is tamed?
Where is the wisdom that makes the difference?

STAGE

The world is a stage, and it plays itself
It boasts of innumerable characters:
Cheaters, murderers, saints...
The performers are the audience
Their roles they play simultaneously
Chaos
Performance so titillating is rewarded with the loudest
Applause.
The hiccup actors get the mouth lashing
The play never ends
Outwitting dictates the tempo
The star performer always
Takes it all

ILLUSIVE WORLD

The world—a vacuum
Drifting, roaming, we exist
Like seasons
We come and go
Like flowers
We blossom in the morning
And die by evening
We are like morning dew that disappears at noon
Yes, we chase shadows
Today we buried four college fellows
They had no chance to blossom
No chance to feel the morning dew
A bus crash ends it all
May their souls rest in peace

TIME BURNS

Our time, like a paper set ablaze, burn
Like an hourglass filters its sand away
It can't be stopped
Make use of it
Before it turns to ashes
Before it filters away
And you will be remembered like a forgotten dream

NO CLUE

Most wonderful stories are yet to be told
The whole truth is yet to be out
What is seen is what is not
What is, is hidden
What you know is no knowledge
Wisdom so cherished maybe no wisdom at all
For non-substance, we struggle and battle to possess
True wisdom, we ignore
Illusion illuminates our world
Far from the truth is the truth we uphold.
What are we to our destinies?
Which life of ours we live out of our choices
Or are they predetermined?
The chaos we swim in daily define our lives
How vast and deep are each of our stories?
So many will never to be told
What am I writing? I do not know
What am I saying? No clue either
What I say is beyond me
But I can't stop now for lack of knowledge
However, little revealed
Is far better than nothing

MY DANCE

I watch the arms of time swiftly passing by
I raise my hands, grabbing only air
I've been inside many valleys
And I've survived uncountable storms
But now
I hear a distant sound
I stand and watch
Could hear some music
I wait
I have been waiting
The music soothes my soul
The time now drags
I wait
The music is clearer and louder
And now
The music is here at last
It is my dance, my victorious dance
I've won at last! I'm an overcomer!

ANOTHER NOTE FROM THE AUTHOR

I hope you enjoyed "Thorns and Roses "
Please check out my upcoming books, "ABC of Making Heaven" and "The Unsung Hero"
For details please visit my website at www.ujuoramah.com
And don't hesitate to drop me a line. I love to hear from you
You can connect with me on my Facebook
https://www.facebook.com/uujuoramah/ and on
http://www.ujuoramah.com/

www.ingramcontent.com/pod-product-compliance
Lightning Source LLC
Chambersburg PA
CBHW071645040426
42452CB00009B/1764